Nº 3
The
North West

by Paul Shannon & John Hillmer

Past and
Present

Past & Present Publishing Ltd

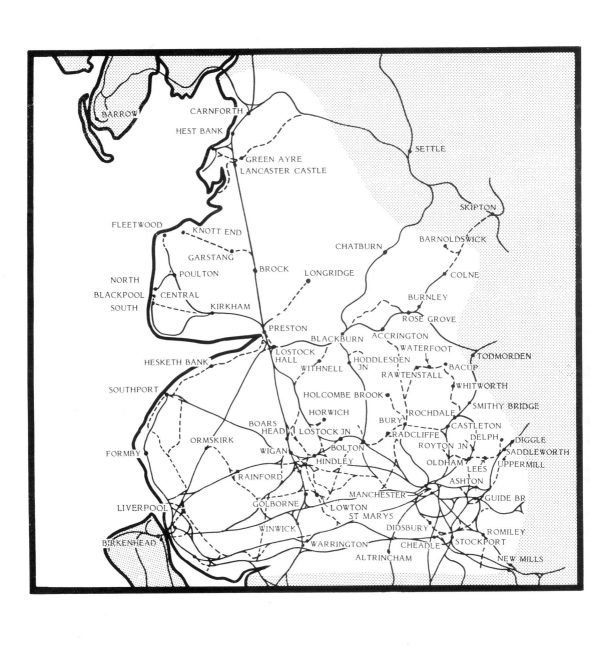

CONTENTS

© Past & Present Publishing/Paul D. Shannon & John C. Hillmer 1986 and 1996

First published in 1986
Reprinted 1988
Reprinted 1991
Reprinted 1992
Reprinted 1996
Reprinted 2002

British Library Cataloguing in Publication Data

A catalogue record for this book is available from the British Library

ISBN 1 85895 097 X

Past & Present Publishing Ltd
The Trundle
Ringstead Road
Great Addington
Kettering
Northants
NN14 4BW

Tel/Fax: 01536 330588
email: sales@nostalgiacollection.com
Website: www.nostalgiacollection.com

Printed and bound in Great Britain

TITLE PAGE: Passing Smithy Bridge station between Rochdale and Todmorden is 'Patriot' 4-6-0 No. 45517 with the 10.30 am Liverpool Exchange-Newcastle Express (one of its regular turns of duty) on September 1 1959. The right-hand poster of the pair on the end of the station's lean-to building announces the planned closure of the station, implemented on May 5 1960. The station was subsequently erased from the landscape, but 24 years later Greater Manchester Council Passenger Transport Executive opened a new halt at Smithy Bridge, as illustrated in the upper picture, as the 0955 Manchester Victoria-York service pauses on January 25 1986. Whereas the platforms of the old station were staggered to minimise road traffic delays, the new halt has both platforms on the western side of the level crossing. *Richard S. Greenwood/PDS.*

INTRODUCTION TO THE FIRST EDITION

THE industrial North West once boasted one of the most complex railway networks in Britain. Today, only a fraction of the former system remains in use, and many of the surviving lines have been reduced in status in some way. For that reason, the task of compiling the North West volume in the 'Past and Present' series has been an especially interesting and rewarding one.

A glance at the map on the inside front cover will indicate to the reader that many line closures were inevitable, simply because duplication of routes occurred when more than one pre-Grouping company sought to gain a foothold in a particular area. Many of the closely interweaving lines around Wigan were built mainly to provide access to collieries, but it would be difficult to justify the building of separate Great Central Railway branches to St. Helens and Wigan Central, or the curiously routed CLC railway system from Widnes and Aintree to Southport Chapel Street. Until comparatively recently, it was possible to travel direct from Liverpool to Manchester by three different routes — those of the CLC, LNWR and LYR companies.

Similarly, it is not surprising that some of the remoter rural branches in the north and east of Lancashire have closed. The railway to the small coastal settlement at Knott End, for example, could never realistically have been a viable proposition. But having said that, the cutbacks during the Beeching era have extended far beyond the elimination of duplicated routes and such obvious 'non-starters' as the Knott End branch. It is sad that the once-extensive network around Bury has now been reduced to a single Manchester-bound route, and that Skipton no longer enjoys direct rail access to East Lancashire, via Colne. Many would say with hindsight that closure of the direct line between Lancaster and Wennington was a mistake, and it is certainly regrettable that the important town and resort of Blackpool has lost its most direct access route, from Kirkham, together with the once thriving terminus at Central.

Whilst in compiling this book we have been made only too aware of the reductions that have been made in the railway system, it is also good to have observed and recorded the results of some recent improvements to both services and facilities. The re-opening to passengers of the Copy Pit line, for example, has reinstated a useful direct link between East Lancashire and Yorkshire; and modern electric units provide an improved service between Liverpool Central and Garston, over a line which actually suffered a period of complete closure. Station re-openings have proved a relatively inexpensive but effective means of attracting new custom to the railway, and we include (on the title page) an interesting pair of views at Smithy Bridge, between Todmorden and Rochdale, where a new halt was opened 24 years after closure of the original LYR station.

We have attempted to present a balanced picture of the changes that have taken place over the years. We have not felt enslaved by a rigidly complete geographical coverage, but have given greater weight to those locations where the change has been considerable or worthy of note in some particular way. In a few cases, where change has been extensive, we had to rely on large scale Ordnance Survey maps or the knowledge of local people to pin-point the exact location of a photograph, whilst at the other extreme, we have included one or two pairings where the change over several decades has been minimal.

We feel greatly indebted to the large number of contributing photographers represented in these pages, both for the loan of material and for assistance with captions. We are equally grateful to the numerous railwaymen who, at all levels, have been sympathetic and helpful to our cause and often shown great interest in the project. Special thanks must go to the Station Managers at Liverpool Lime Street and Blackburn for particular assistance at these locations. Finally, we hope that the reader will find the same pleasure in reading this book as we found in compiling it, and perhaps share some of the excitement of standing in exactly the same spot as another photographer did 20 or 30 years ago.

PAUL SHANNON & JOHN HILLMER
September, 1986.

Opposite page, top: **Climbing between Central and Mumps stations in Oldham, a pair of Stanier 4-6-0s, Nos. 45339 and 44816 head north with a lengthy excursion train on Sunday July 28 1963. All down excursions on the Oldham branch were double-headed because of the gradients between Thorpes Bridge Junction and the line summit near Royton Junction. Oldham Central station, just visible in the background, closed on April 18 1966. To the left were extensive sidings which were used for the 1960 parcels concentration depot, but with the closure of this facility in May 1981, the railway was reduced to no more than two parallel tracks, as illustrated in the March 1986 view of 'Pacer' unit No. 142035 on a morning Rochdale-Manchester Victoria working. As the railway has declined, the road has increased in importance.** *R.S. Greenwood/PDS.*

CARNFORTH

Above: In early diesel days, English Electric Type 4 (later class 40) No. D325 heads the down 'Royal Scot' through Carnforth station in 1961. The main line platforms here were closed on May 4 1970 and subsequently removed, leaving only the Furness line platforms, still used today by the Barrow and Leeds services. Thus, curiously, Carnforth is physically situated on the West Coast Main Line, yet without the possibility of main line trains stopping there. The goods yard (on the left), semaphore signals, water columns and signal box have all disappeared, to be replaced by the intricacy of electrification masts and wires, as seen in the modern shot of No.86206 (right) hauling the 1110 Birmingham-Edinburgh/Inverness of April 7 1986. The class 40s are now extinct from capital stock and No. D325, renumbered 40125 under the TOPS scheme, was withdrawn in May 1981. It was scrapped at Swindon Works in December 1983. *W.H. Ashcroft/ PDS.*

Left: In this overall view of Carnforth Yard in February 1958, Fowler '4F' 0-6-0 No. 44192 blows off before leaving with a freight for Barrow-in-Furness. Meanwhile, on the right, a 'Jinty' 0-6-0T shunts assorted wagons and vans in what is now Steamtown's car park, as illustrated in the modern view, (below) on April 17 1986. *W.H. Ashcroft/ PDS.*

HEST BANK is the location for this August 22 1954 view (top) of Stanier 4-6-2 No. 46206 *Princess Marie Louise* running south with a Glasgow-Euston express. This was a Sunday and the train was following the up 'Royal Scot', in the happy days when there was enough traffic to justify two full-length expresses running about 30 minutes apart. Since the 'past' picture was taken, the semaphore signals have gone and the signal box itself survives only as a level crossing frame, the regulation of trains being taken over by Preston power box in 1973.

The station was closed on February 3 1969, the platforms being removed during electrification of the West Coast Main Line. The single line spur from Bare Lane Station was extended over the site of the down platform at the same time, the junction being re-sited adjacent to the level crossing and signal box. Above: A latter day view of the same location as No. 85002 passes with an afternoon train from Edinburgh and Glasgow to Cardiff on April 7 1986. *Robert Leslie/PDS.*

THESE two pictures illustrate the changes affecting the West Coast Main Line and its traffic at Lancaster Castle Station, opened in 1846 by the Lancaster & Carlisle Railway Company. In the upper picture, unique Riddles '8P' 4-6-2 No. 71000 Duke of Gloucester sprints south on the up fast line with a Glasgow-Birmingham express of August 21 1954. Lancaster No. 4 signalbox is visible in the distance, whilst the catenary masts mark the course of the electrified Lancaster-Morecambe-Heysham line, which diverged sharply to the right, to Green Ayre Station. Below: On April 7 1986 Class 86 electric loco-motives Nos. 86419 and 86422 take the up fast with a southbound steel coil train — a traffic known locally to railwaymen as 'the watchsprings:' Paradoxically, the catenary first installed by the Midland Railway has gone and the Green Ayre line itself closed, a truncated section being retained for stock storage — the bufferstop is just out of sight beyond the trees. Semaphore signalling and the LNWR signalboxes were superseded by the commissioning of Preston power box in 1973, whilst electrified passenger services between Preston and Carlisle started on May 6 1974. *Robert Leslie/PDS.*

THE overall main line layout at Lancaster Castle station has remained essentially unchanged over the years, apart from the inevitable loss of semaphore signalling, signal boxes, gas lighting and other period detail. Nearly 23 years separate these two views of northbound departing expresses — Stanier three-cylinder 'Jubilee' 4-6-0 No. 45574 *India* in July 1963, and class 86 No. 86220 *Goliath* with a Nottingham-Glasgow/ Edinburgh service of April 7 1986. The branch to Glasson Dock diverges to the left in front of No.45574, which was withdrawn from service in March 1966 and placed in store at Leeds Holbeck shed (55A). It was scrapped by Draper's of Hull in August 1966. *Ken Roberts/PDS.*

GREEN AYRE was the Midland Railway station at Lancaster, its services running along the now-closed Lune Valley line to Wennington Junction as well as to Morecambe and Heysham. It was the latter route which was chosen as early as 1908 for a pilot electrification scheme which lasted until 1951, when the line was converted to 50Hz operation (25 kv), using rebuilt LNWR stock which was already 40 years old. One of these units is illustrated (top) at Green Ayre in 1960. Green Ayre station and its link to Wennington disappeared from the passenger network on January 3 1966 and this area is now a riverside park. It is hard to believe from the modern 1986 view that a railway ever existed here. *W.H. Ashcroft/Steve Lister.*

Right: Looking east from Skerton Bridge, Lancaster, it is difficult to believe that the Green Ayre-Wennington link ever existed: the location is occupied today by a pedestrian walkway and a light industrial development. It was a very different view on July 30 1963 (below) as Ivatt '2MT' 2-6-0 No. 46441 (now preserved at Steamtown, Carnforth) left Ladies Walk Sidings with Target 73, the 2.45pm New Zealand Sidings — Heysham Moss. Closed to passengers on January 3 1966, this line remained open for freight until June 5 1967. Many observers feel that this link should have been retained, rather than the longer Furness & Midland Joint line from Wennington to Carnforth. *Ron Herbert/PDS.*

Above: A delightful scene at Halton-on-Lune, on the MR line between Lancaster Green Ayre and Wennington Junction, as Sulzer Type 2 (later Class 25) diesel-electric No. D 7597 passes with the 12.35am Morecambe-Leeds service of September 25 1964. The locomotive is in early BR two-tone green livery, whilst the rake of mixed BR Mk1 and LMS coaches is painted maroon. The list of tolls next to the crossing includes charges of 1d for cycles, 'foot passengers' and 'riding horses' whilst horse drawn carts cost 1½d, cattle 3d per score and motor cars and horse drawn carriages 3d each. It was in the interest of farmers to take pigs, calves and sheep across in large numbers — a single animal was charged at 1d, whilst a dozen animals cost just 1½d! To look at the woodland car park occupying this site in August 1986, you would never know the railway had ever been here. It was closed to passengers in January 1966. *Noel Machell/Steve Lister.*

Above: Hughes-Fowler 'Crab' 2-6-0 No. 42893 stands out of use, on August 22 1961, at Lancaster Green Ayre shed, adjacent to Green Ayre station, at the foot of the sharply-curved and steeply-graded single track line which connected with the West Coast Main Line at Lancaster Castle, (see page 9). The single-ended shed had four roads, access to the shed in the cramped yard being via the turntable. In LMS days Green Ayre housed less than 30 locomotives, though this figure had risen to almost 40 by the early 1940s. Green Ayre was coded variously from MR days as 32, M32, MC, 20H, 23C, ME 24J, and finally 10J, which it retained until closure on April 18 1966. The shed building survived in modified form as the New Planet City youth centre until the mid 1980s, when it was demolished to make way for a Sainsbury's supermarket and car park, as illustrated (below in the August 1986 picture. All that remains to positively identify the location in the 1980s is the tree on horizon, visible on the right. *Ron Herbert/Steve Lister*

Top: On July 25 1963, Stanier class 5MT 4-6-0 No. 45135, of Springs Branch shed, shunts at Garstang Town station, the decaying remains of the headquarters of the Garstang & Knott End Railway, which diverged from the West Coast Main Line north of Garstang & Catterall station. The train was known locally as the 'Pilling Pig' and was the daily freight from Preston (Ribble Sidings) to Pilling, by then the terminus of the truncated line, until its final closure on August 16 1965.

Above: A housing estate occupies the site today and whilst it was a pleasant gesture to retain the memory of the railway by an appropriate naming of the approach road, this must be extremely confusing to newcomers, as the nearest railway (the WCML) is some distance away! *W.H. Ashcroft/JCH.*

THE Garstang & Knott End Railway terminated at the coastal hamlet of Knott End, on the estuary of the River Wyre. Knott End Station is pictured (above) with two trains at the platforms. Construction of the GKNR was over-optimistic and run-down of the branch commenced as early as 1930 when the passenger trains were withdrawn between Garstang Town and Knott End.

Freight services were cut back to Pilling in 1950, t Garstang Town in 1963, and the entire branch wa closed on August 16 1965. Now all that remains at Kno End is the station building, currently in use as a caf The modern picture (below) was taken on August 1986. *The Sankey Collection/JCH.*

Above: Brock water troughs, between Preston and Lancaster, are the location for this view of Fowler 2-6-4T No. 42312, running briskly north with an excursion from Crewe to Windermere, composed entirely of LMS stock. The date was July 20 1963, and on the left of the picture can be seen the earthworks for the construction of the M6 Motorway. Note the locomotive boiler, in use at the trackside as a water tank for supplying the troughs. Today the motorway is obscured by mature trees and the railway has been modernised, as shown in the 1986 view (left) of a class 85-hauled Euston-Glasgow express. *Ian G. Holt/ PDS.*

BLACKPOOL
AND THE FYLDE

THIS page & opposite: A pair of pictures for which words of adequate descriptive power are difficult to find. In 1947, when the older picture was taken from the top of Blackpool Tower (518 ft), it would have been considered inconceivable that Blackpool Central station's 14 platforms would be swept away to make way for car and coach parks, and an amusement complex. Central station, at the end of the direct line serving the resort, from Kirkham, was closed on November 2 1964, and even local railway men could not understand how the heavy volume of traffic, especially during the summer, would subsequently be accomodated at the town's North and South stations. The main line trackbed from Blackpool Central (and Blackpool South) has been used as the foundation for an extension of the M55 motorway and is used for bringing cars and coaches to the parking areas constructed on the station site itself in recent years. Note that the glazed-roofed toilet block is the only part of the station to survive in July 1986, when the modern picture was taken. In the 1947 scene, the trains are (right to left): the 4pm to Manchester Victoria (eight coaches plus one van), hauled by '5MT' 4-6-0 No. 4778; the 5.5pm to Euston (10 coaches) with 'Jubilee'4-6-0 No. 5574 *India;* four empty coaches (on a centre road) due to leave for Accrington at 5.55pm, the 4.35pm for Bolton (five coaches) with 2-6-4T No. 2435; the 7.21pm to Leeds City South (seven coaches); the 7pm to Manchester Victoria, via Marton (eight coaches); the 6pm return to Southport Chapel Street, via Marton, (six coaches, plus one vehicle against the bufferstop) and the 8pm to Blackburn, via Marton (five coaches). On the extreme left are three sets of spare coaches for use as required. Just visible in front of the toilet block are the LYR 0-4-4Ts, used as stationary boilers for carriage heating. *Frank Dean/ Nigel Harris.*

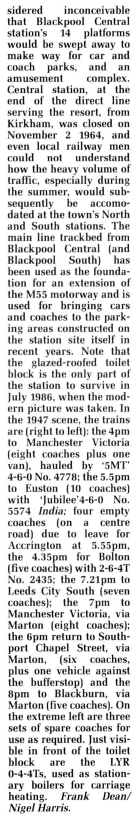

Top: A very busy scene at Blackpool Central station throat on July 22 1963, pictured from the roof of one of the power station buildings, visible adjacent to the main line in the centre distance on page 18: these buildings too are long gone. Stanier 'Jubilee' 4-6-0 No. 45695 *Minotaur* makes an aggresive start with a Leeds train, as Stanier '5MT' 4-6-0 No. 45304 rolls towards the platforms with a service from Manchester Victoria. Awaiting departure in the station is Class 5 No. 45216 with a train for Halifax.

Below: A similar viewpoint in July 1986, and all trace of the railway has gone, the formation now used by the M55 extension and the coach park. The large flat-roofed building in the centre background is the former engine men's lodging barracks, now abandoned. It is difficult to believe that such an extensive railway location could be so completely obliterated — and the logic of closing the railway in order to facilitate increased road traffic is highly dubious, to say the least! *Frank Dean/Nigel Harris.*

op: In the summer months especially, Blackpool Central shed was a magnificent location for the railway photo-
rapher and 'loco-spotter' with a wide variety of motive power from many distant locations arriving on a range of
xcursions and 'extras'. The shed is pictured here on June 15 1963, just over a year before closure, as host to '5MT'
o. 44833, Hughes-Fowler 'Crab' 2-6-0 No. 42721, Riddles 'Britannia Pacific' No. 70016 *Ariel*, Stanier '8F' 2-8-0 No.
8315, and 'Black 5s' No. 45315 and double chimney-fitted No. 44766. BR rebuilt the shed with a new steel-framed
oof, with glazing and smoke troughs, in 1957/8, but closure followed on November 2 1964. The shed site is now used
s a coach park, as illustrated (above) in July 1986. *Frank Dean/Nigel Harris.*

Top: On August 18 1962, Stanier 'Jubilee' 4-6-0 No. 45590 *Travancore* is turned manually at Blackpool South, who[se] carriage sidings were frequently filled to capacity with excursion stock on busy Summer Saturdays in the 1950s an[d] early 1960s. Above: In 1986 no trace of the turntable survived in the wasteland once occupied by sidings, whilst th[e] main line formation in front of the terraced houses now carries a footpath and the M55 extension to the car/coac[h] parks on the Central station site. *Frank Dean/PDS.*

Top: Blackpool South, situated approximately one mile from the terminus at Blackpool Central, was a through station where the direct line to the West Coast Main Line, via Kirkham, curved inland, away from the longer coastal route to Kirkham, via Lytham. In the older picture, Stanier three-cylinder 'Jubilee' 4-6-0 No. 45653 *Barham* is rolling into platform 1 at Blackpool South, from the coastal line, with a Bletchley-Blackpool working of June 20 1959. Above: A similar view of the same location in 1986, though from a slightly lower level, as the footbridge from which the 1959 picture was taken has long gone, while the footpath and neatly tended gardens have disappeared beneath unkempt undergrowth. The extensive sidings beyond the signal box have been lifted to provide yet another car/coach park adjacent to the M55 extension, built on the former 'direct' line trackbed which was further over to the left. This once extensive through station survived in 1986 only as a single track, single platform terminus, operated by a DMU shuttle from Kirkham. *Frank Dean/PDS.*

THIS IS another pair of pictures which graphically illustrate how roads frequently gain precedence over railways in the formation of long term transport plans. Above: On May 23 1964 Riddles 'Clan' 4-6-0 No. 72007 *Clan Mackintosh* passes Marton, heading for Blackpool Central on the direct line from Kirkham, as part of the day's itinerary for the RCTS Ribble-Lune Railtour. Although the Blackpool South-Kirkham direct line closed to regular services on September 7 1964, it remained in occasional use for summer Saturday 'extras' until September 3 1966. Below: A view of the same location in July 1986, and the railway has given way to the M55 motorway, which carries road traffic over the railway formation to the car and coach park on the Central station site. A single average sized train probably carries the equivalent of about 100 car loads or six coach loads of road-borne visitors and the railway is far more energy-efficient and less environmentally harmful than a constant procession of cars, coaches and lorries, and yet . . . *Frank Dean/Nigel Harris*

HE railway situation at Blackpool North in the 1980s is not as grim as this pair of pictures apparently indicates, or part of the station (the former excursion platforms, located off to the left of this scene) are still in use with good passenger links to Preston and the Anglo-Scottish main line. The main part of the station (illustrated below) was closed and the track, platforms and build-ings swept away to make room for town centre redeve-lopment, including a large supermarket. On July 6 1965, Stanier 'Jubilee' 4-6-0 No. 45627 *Sierra Leone* enters the platforms with a train from Liverpool Exchange. This location today is in use as a car park and taxi rank: the 'new' station entrance and concourse is off to the left, (below). *Frank Dean/PDS.*

BLACKPOOL North shed, known as 'Talbot Road' until 1933/4, was opened in the middle 1880s and was secondary in importance to the larger Blackpool Central shed, and crews worked from either depot as required. Like Central shed, Blackpool North received a new glazed steel-framed roof in 1957/8, only to close in the mid 1960s. Above: pictured on   shed at 'North shed' on September 19 1966 are Stanier '5MT' 4-6-0 No. 45254 and Riddles 'Britannia Pacific' No. 70022 *Tornado* whose name has been painted on the deflector plate following removal of the cast plate. Below: The same location in July 1986 presented a sad sight indeed: the shed building has been obliterated from the landscape and only a couple of little-used and rusty sidings survive in the rubbish littering the wasteland next to the coal depot. *Frank Dean/Nigel Harris.*

THIS pair of pictures illustrate the arm of the triangle at Poulton-le-Fylde which allowed trains to run direct between Blackpool and Fleetwood. Above: On May 10 1953 '4MT' 2-6-4T No. 42481 is beside the platforms at Poulton Curve Halt, which closed to passengers on December 1 1952. This arm of the triangle (between Poulton No. 4 and No. 5 signalboxes) survived however until November 2 1964, the same day that Blackpool Central closed. The Poulton-Fleetwood line is visible in the fields in the background. Left: The trackbed at Poulton Curve Halt is now used as a footpath, and little trace of the once-neat station remains. Residential development has encroached on the agricultural land in the background. *Frank Dean/ Nigel Harris.*

Right top: An overall view of the impressive terminus at Fleetwood, looking towards the bufferstops, on May 19 1964 as Riddles 2-6-2T No. 84016 arrives with a two-coach local train. The railway linking Fleetwood with the North Union Railway, at Preston, was authorised by Act of Parliament in 1835 and opened on July 15 1840, as part of a grand plan to make the Fylde coast town an important staging post on an envisaged Anglo-Scottish trunk route involving both rail and maritime transport. To emphasise this aim, a large sea-front hotel was named 'The North Euston', but these ambitions were never realised and Fleetwood was developed instead as a seaside resort and fishing port. The station at Fleetwood closed on April 18 1966, when the passenger link to Poulton le Fylde was withdrawn. The station was subsequently demolished and the site is now used by the Pandoro company in connection with its Anglo-Irish roll-on-roll-off freight operations. Below: The imposing, if austere, station frontage on June 26 1965. *John Marshall/Nigel Harris.*

PRESTON
AND DISTRICT

ORIGINALLY built to carry stone from Longridge Fell to Preston, the single-track railway to Longridge was completed in 1839 and opened to traffic in 1840, with all trains originally being horse-drawn. Locomotive haulage started on June 12 1848, and passenger services from Preston (Maudlands) to Longridge began on November 1 1856. The Preston & Longridge Railway remained independent until 1867, when it was incorporated into the LNWR/LYR systems. Passenger traffic to Longridge ceased in 1930, although freight continued until 1967. Above: On September 22 1962 LNWR 'Super D' 0-8-0 No. 49451 prepares to return to Preston, at Longridge, with an RCTS railtour comprised entirely of LMS stock. The station was behind the photographer. Following closure of the branch the trackbed was used to create an access road to a new housing development (left). *P.J. Fitton/JCH.*

THE changing face of the 'East Lancashire' side of Preston station, whose trains travelled via Todd Lane Junction to Bamber Bridge, and thence to the Lancashire towns of Blackburn, Accrington and Burnley. Construction of this part of Preston station in the mid-1800s had been fraught with difficulties, disagreement and hostility which was eventually settled by no less a person than Isambard Kingdom Brunel! When the ELR had first come to Preston, the town Corporation had objected to the idea of a second crossing of the Ribble, and the new line had to join the existing North Union railway metals at Farington Junction, $2\frac{1}{2}$ miles south of the station, and services started from Blackburn in 1846. However, obstructive tactics by the NUR regarding access to its station at Preston prompted the ELR to seek independent access. A direct route from Bamber Bridge was surveyed as early as 1846, despite strong opposition from Preston Corporation and the NUR. This was ignored by Parliament which approved the ELR's proposals on July 22 1847. However the ELR was to provide a public park on the Northern bank of the new Ribble crossing and the new bridge was to carry a footpath in addition to the railway. The Act also stipulated that the NUR should extend its station to accommodate the new services within 18 months. However, eight years of

bickering over costs and shared responsibility followed until Brunel was called in to arbitrate in 1856. The new line was eventually opened from Bamber Bridge on September 2 1850. The 'EL' side of the station was subsequently extended in 1913, when two bays and two through further platforms were added. Facing page; top: A fine panoramic view of the 'EL' platforms from East Cliff on May 18 1968 as Riddles *'Britannia'* 4-6-2 No. 70013 *Oliver Cromwell* leaves with an excursion for Carnforth. Butler Street goods yard is on the right. Facing page, below: A similar view of the same location on April 2 1986. Following closure of Butler Street Goods (1972) and the Preston EL-Bamber Bridge link (1972) this land has been developed chiefly as a car park both for rail users and shoppers using the new development visible in the right background. Butler Street has also been widened to provide easy access both to the car parks and the new pedestrian station access provided in 1986 on the site of the former EL booking office. *John S. Whiteley/JCH.* Above: The sharply curved 'EL' approach to Preston, viewed from the former platform 6 as 'Patriot' 4-6-0 No. 45515 *Caernavon* rolls in with the 6.30pm Southport-Blackpool of July 4 1960. *W.H. Ashcroft.*

Right: A view of Preston's current platform 1, looking south, on July 16 1986, as a Manchester-Blackpool DMU prepares to depart. The platform on which the photographer is standing was in 1986 used only for parcels traffic, though it was formerly platform No.2. The trackwork in the centre of the picture and a barely visible flight of steps on the left are all that link this view to the older picture (below) which shows this part of Preston station circa 1912. *JCH.*

IN 1912 Preston was a 'joint station' with six platforms straddling the LNWR Anglo-Scottish main line, with a further three platforms serving East Lancashire (see pages 30-31). LYR traffic joined the main line south of Preston at Euxton Junction, trains from both Manchester and Liverpool to Blackpool and Fleetwood normally using platform 1 (off to the right of this field of view), while traffic from the Fylde to Manchester or Liverpool usually used platform 2. Platforms 1-6 were covered by the impressive overall roof, and note the smoke boards above the running lines.The lattice footbridge linked the booking office with the platforms. Several station 'pilots' were always in attendance, this 2-4-2T being one of the LYR engines continuously on duty. One of it duties was to take the direct portion of the Manchester Blackpool 'Club' train forward from Preston to Black pool Central, via Marton, whilst the train engine took the longer route via Lytham and St. Annes. The white 'A' indicated the required route to signalmen en route the main train carried a 'B' code. The overall roof wa cut back in 1960. *Lancashire & Yorkshire Railwa Society's Collections.*

Above: Farington Junction is the location for this picture of Riddles 'WD' 2-8-0 No. 90667, heading north with a train of empty bogie bolster wagons on April 24 1962. Since that time, the up and down sidings have all been removed and the Farington Link Road now crosses the railway just beyond the site of the former signal box. The modern view (below) shows class 47 No.47011 passing the same spot with a northbound 'Speedlink' working on June 18 1986. *V.H. Ashcroft/PDS.*

Awaiting the cutting torch at Lostock Hall in December 1967 are three Ivatt '4MT' 2-6-0s including Nos. 43004 and 43046, together with a selection of Stanier locomotives. No. 43004 had been withdrawn from traffic in September 1967 and was towed to Cohen's yard at Kettering shortly after this picture was taken: it was scrapped in February 1968. No. 43046 had been withdrawn in the previous month, and remained in store at this shed until January 1968 after which it was towed to Motherwell Machinery & Scrap Company, where it was scrapped in February 1968. Lostock Hall closed as a steam depot on August 5 1968, though it remained in use for maintenance and fuelling of diesel traction, and was used subsequently by BR's Carriage & Wagon Department. The building and some track survived into the second half of the 1980s, but by 14 June 1995 (centre) all had been flattened. The shed opened in 1882 and in the 1930s was host to 60 locomotives. *W. H. Ashcroft/JCH.*

Right below: Stanier '5MT' 4-6-0 No. 44888 is the centre of attention at Lostock Hall on July 21 1968. *Ian G. Holt.*

Above: Adjacent to Lostock Hall shed was Lostock Hall station, pictured here in wintry weather on a Sunday in 1967 as an unidentified Brush Type 4 (later class 47) passes with a Liverpool/Manchester-Glasgow service, diverted via Blackburn, Hellifield and the Settle-Carlisle line. The station closed in 1969 and has since been completely erased, together with much of the motive power depot's equipment, as illustrated (left) on March 28 1986 as a DMU passes Lostock Hall forming a Preston-Colne service. A new station has been opened at Lostock Hall (see page 36) *W.H. Ashcroft/JCH.*

Top: Stanier class 8F 2-8-0 No. 48077 threads its way across Lostock Hall Junction with empty 16-ton mineral wagons from Preston to Rose Grove in December 1967. The locomotive is alongside the former wagon repair shops, which were situated behind Lostock Hall Junction signal box, and were closed at the same time as the MPD in August 1968. Above: A similar view of Lostock Hall Junction on April 2 1986 as a four-car Class 108 DMU approaches the new Lostock Hall station, opened with the assistance of Lancashire County Council on May 14 1984. The original station was on the other side of the bridge. *W.H. Ashcroft/JCH.*

AROUND
BLACKBURN

Top: The writing was already on the wall for Withnell station in 1959 when LMS class 4MT Stanier 2-6-4T No. 42473 called to pick up one or two passengers on the Blackburn-Wigan 'local'. This line, from Cherry Tree to Chorley (closed on January 4 1960) produced a varied selection of motive power, and even Riddles '9F' 2-10-0s were recorded occasionally. Close examination of the old picture reveals a diminutive Austin A30 saloon parked on the approach road; this car was then four years old and had been bought by the photographer for £423-10-0 in 1958! The latter-day view (above) taken in April 1986, shows the station building and platforms to be well maintained. Trains continue to use the station, for the new owner has even added a miniature railway linking the platforms! *N.R.Knight/PDS.*

HODDLESDEN JUNCTION lies between Blackburn and Darwen, and until 1950 was junction for the freight-only branch to Hoddlesden village. Above: 'Britannia' 4-6-2 No. 70015 *Apollo* heads south with an RCTS railtour on March 19 1967. Below: The same scene on April 6 1986, with 'Pacer' unit No. 142030 forming the 1440 Blackburn-Manchester service. The line on the left serves the Reeds paper mill siding, which was used by regular oil traffic until mid-1985, with subsequent deliveries only as required. *I.G. Holt/PDS.*

Left, above: Stanier '3MT' 2-6-2T No. 40120 stands in the Manchester bay at Blackburn station with the 3.45 departure for Victoria on August 25 1955. This scene has changed significantly, and not were the gas lights and platform canopy removed but the entire platform disappeared, as shown (left, below) on March 29 1986. The unusual appearance of a locomotive-hauled passenger train on that date was a consequence of engineering work on the West Coast Main Line north of Preston; thus Class 47 No. 47562 was heading the diverted 0945 Glasgow/0940 Edinburgh-Poole working. On the left is a class 142 'Pacer' unit awaiting departure to Manchester - then the most recent generation of local train and a direct descendant of the train in the old shot. *Brian Morrison/ PDS.*

Right: Midland Railway 0-6-0 No. 44460 stands beneath the overall roof at Blackburn with the 10.19 am to Hellifield on May 13 1961. A highly evocative scene. *I. G. Holt.*

Above: At the east end of Blackburn station Stanier class 5MT No.45227 arrives with a Liverpool-bound express on August 25 1955. In comparison, the modern view (right) shows a class 108 DMU departing with a Preston-Leeds service on March 29 1986. The trackwork was radically altered during the resignalling scheme of Autumn 1973, during which all of Blackburn's passenger facililties were concentrated on the north-ernmost island platform. Other unused platform faces were cut back. The 'Daniel Thwaites Mineral Water Depot' above the tunnel mouth has been taken over by Blackburn shoe retailer Tommy Ball. *Brian Morrison/PDS.*

HE link from Daisyfield Junction (Blackburn) to Helli-
eld survives in the mid-1980s as a double track railway
r use by one or two freight services and as an import-
nt diversionary route. During engineering work or
verhead supply faults on the West Coast Main Line
orth of Preston, Anglo-Scottish services run between
arington Junction, Blackburn, Hellifield and the Settle-
arlisle line. One of these diversions is illustrated

(above) as class 47 No. 47442 heads south through the
disused station at Chatburn with the 1105 Glasgow-
Euston express of March 29 1986. Below: Fairburn Class
4MT 2-6-4T No. 42154 pauses at the tidy but little-used
station at Chatburn, with a three-coach local train
bound for Blackburn. Passenger services were withdrawn between Blackburn and Hellifield on September
10 1962. *N.R. Knight/PDS.*

EAST LANCASHIRE

ACCRINGTON was the junction for the LYR line to Ramsbottom and Bury, which is seen on the right of the older picture (above) and this route was closed on December 5 1966, except for a short siding at Accrington used for parcels traffic for a further few years. A class 110 three-car DMU, in original green livery complete with front-end yellow 'cats whiskers,' is seen arriving on a Bradford-Blackpool service on March 28 1963. Right: A class 108 DMU of similar vintage, but in more up-to-date blue livery, forms the 1438 Leeds-Preston service on March 1 1986. The signal box and semaphore signalling were made redundant in 1973 by the commissioning of Preston Power Box which controls the line from Preston to Eastwood. *L. Kay/PDS.*

Top: Approaching Rose Grove from the west is Stanier Class 8F 2-8-0 No. 48730 with the 8.35 am Wyre Dock-Healey Mills coal empties, on May 7 1968. Plentiful coal traffic from the West Yorkshire coalfield to the Lancashire power stations traversed this route well into the 1970s, whereas today there are no regular freight services at all, at the time of writing. The modern view of a Preston-Colne DMU (above), taken on March 1 1986, shows the junction for Padiham still in situ, though oil trains to the power station at the end of the branch are few and far between. This junction was at one end of the Padiham 'loop' which rejoined the line to Preston at Blackburn (Great Harwood Junction). Blackburn-Rose Grove passenger services (via Padiham) were withdrawn on December 2 1957, though the link remained in situ for seasonal and excursion trains until complete closure in summer 1963. The Padiham-Blackburn section was lifted. *J.S. Whiteley/PDS.*

ROSE GROVE engine shed was opened by the Lanca-shire & Yorkshire Railway in 1899 as 'Shed No. 23', and survived as a working steam depot until August 5 1968, seven days before the very last steam train ran on British Rail metals. The older picture was taken on August 20 1968, when diesels were using two roads of the six-road shed, and all remaining roads were full of redundant Stanier 2-8-0s and '5MT' 4-6-0s. When with-drawn the connecting rods were dismantled and not cut from the locomotives as was the case at many other sheds. The last engine to leave Rose Grove for the scrapyard was 'Black Five' No. 44899, in December 1968. It was towed away and scrapped by Cohen's of Kettering, in January 1969. Rose Grove was coded 24B under Accrington, from 1935 until September 1963 when it became 10F. Now, as illustrated above, the whole site is barely recognisable, having given way to the M65 Motorway! *Mike Taylor/PDS.*

THREE generations of signalling are illustrated on this page at Burnley's Gannow Junction, where the Copy Pit and Colne lines diverge. Above left: Stanier '5MT' 4-6-0 No. 44863 takes the Copy Pit route during 1956, when the original LYR signal box, visible in the background, was still in use. Above right: Newly built in front of the original signal box is the 'new' box, completed in 1964, and which only lasted nine years until the Preston Power Box re-signalling scheme reached this area.

Below: A class 108 DMU runs over the simplified junction to the Colne line on March 1 1986, and approaches the point giving access to the double track section to Nelson, from where the line was then single track to Colne; singling of the Gannow-Nelson section has since taken place. *N. Harling/L. Kay/PDS.*

Above: Burnley Central station was a hive of activity in 1951, when this fine overall view looking west was taken. A 2-4-2T in charge of a two coach local train is just departing, the goods sidings on the right are full with varied freight traffic, and on the left can be seen the sidings leading to Bank Hall Colliery, which was three-quarters of a mile away and had its own steam shunting locomotive. In contrast, the modern picture shows how much the railway has diminished in recent times, with only a simple, modernised passenger station remaining. Below: A pair of two-car class 108 DMUs are seen departing on the 0736 Preston-Colne service on March 29 1986; the goods yard is abandoned and the colliery exchange sidings site is now occupied by a public park area. Note too the much reduced number of mill chimneys in the town beyond the station. *N. Harling/PDS.*

COLNE marked the end of Lancashire & Yorkshire Railway metals, and the line towards Skipton was operated by the Midland Railway. This explains the Midland Railway Standard signal box just north of the station, as seen in the upper picture of Stanier class 5MT 4-6-0 No. 45386 arriving with a westbound evening parcels train on June 13 1968. Whilst the LYR section from Burnley remains in use, to a much simplified terminus at Colne (immediately behind the photographer) the Skipton line was completely closed on February 2 1970 and subsequently demolished, as the April 1986 view clearly shows. Notice, incidentally, the variety of parcels stock which includes SR, BR standard and LMS vehicles at the head of the train. *R.H. Short/PDS.*

BARNOLDSWICK was the terminus of a Midland Railway branch from Earby, on the Colne-Skipton line, and remained in use until 1965. Above: BR Riddles class 2MT 2-6-2T No. 84015 at Barnoldswick after arrival with the 4.15pm Earby-Barnoldswick special working of June 22 1963. Inspection of the timetable for 1964 reveals a most curious arrangement of train services — arrivals at 11.59 (SO) from Earby and 16.49 (SX) from Skipton and departures at 08.19 (EWD) to Skipton and 17,00 (SX) to Skipton! Today, the station approach has been landscaped, and nothing remains of the railway itself. *Ian G.Holt/PDS.*

TO
SOUTHPORT

THE direct route from Southport to Preston, originally built by the West Lancashire Railway, served a number of small communities including Hesketh Bank, which is pictured with a Riddles class 4 4-6-0 No. 75047 arriving with a morning Southport-Preston train on September 1 1964. This was the final week of passenger services on this route, which closed on September 7 1964. The other two pictures show the same location on May 10 1969 and March 28 1986 — illustrating a sequence of events all too often witnessed after the cutbacks of Beeching era.
John Marshall/JCH.

Right, above: This view from the footbridge between Southport's Chapel Street and St. Luke's stations on July 23 1960 shows Stanier class 5 No. 45442 at the head of the 4.12pm train for Preston, with the junction signal cleared for the line towards Meols Cop. LYR 2-4-2T No. 50850 acts as station pilot on the right in front of the engine shed yard, whilst class 5MT No. 45042 (left) reverses out of the station ready to move on to the shed for coal and water. In the modern view, taken on April 18 1986, a class 110 diesel multiple unit is seen departing on the 1215 service to Manchester, with 'Steamport' (the former engine shed) clearly visible on the right. *R.S. Greenwood/JCH.*

Below: Chapel Street station on August 24 1961, with LYR 2-4-2 'Radial' tank No. 50850 in charge of a train empty stock. *I.G. Holt.*

Top: Formby station, looking towards Southport, probably in August 1904. The train is a three-car set of the original clerestory 'wedge-end' stock, the operating number '11' on the white board identifiying it as an afternoon 'all stations' to Southport. Note the signs along the platforms, indicating to passengers where the different classes of accommodation in the trains could be found. Liverpool commuters are provided with a canopy whose valances are painted in the usual LYR style — alternate boards in tan and brown. Formby was a passenger-only station with no goods facilities. The latter-day view (above) shows the scene on April 18 1986 as class 507 EMU No. 507003 departs for South-port. *Lancashire and Yorkshire Society's Collections/ JCH.*

RAILS TO
LIVERPOOL

Right, above: An interesting view of Ormskirk station, on the Preston-Liverpool line, circa 1910, when the station had full passenger and goods facilities and enjoyed branch services to Skelmersdale in addition to main line trains to both Liverpool and Preston. An immaculate LYR railmotor is standing in the bay on the right, including a trailer coach of the type attached at busy periods. A Skelmersdale branch train is visible at one of the main platforms whilst a rake of mixed goods wagons are standing on the left. *Lancashire and Yorkshire Railway Society's Collections.*

Right: Stanier '5MT' 4-6-0 No. 45424 departs for Liverpool Exchange with a train from Blackpool on October 1 1962, whilst a local EMU stands in the bay on the right. *R.S. Greenwood.*

Left: Ormskirk on April 1986 with class 508 EMU No. 508143 awaiting departure for Liverpool. This is a much-simplified scene: the bay platform and the goods facilities are long gone and through services no longer operate through the station. The single track DMU service from Preston meets end-on with EMU services to Liverpool and a buffer stop located half-way along the platform separates the two systems. The track on the left provides a through link for emergency purposes only. *PD.*

Above: Just north of Sandhills junction on the Aintree line, a 1938-built class 502 electric unit is seen on an afternoon Ormskirk-Liverpool Exchange working on February 26 1966. At that time Bank Hall locomotive shed was situated just to the left of the picture. The later view shows class 507 EMU No. 507015 on a Kirkby-Garston service, on April 1 1986, by which time the tunnel between Moorfields and Central had allowed operation of through services to the south of the city. The sidings on the left now form part of Kirkdale EMU depot, whilst the expanse of CLC tracks on the right have long since disappeared. *Ian G. Holt/PDS*

Below, left: On August 26 1966, Rainford Junction was still the meeting point of three routes. Straight ahead is the line to Liverpool, on the left is the former LNWR line to St. Helens (closed to passengers from June 18 1951), and on the right is the former ELR Skelmersdale branch to Ormskirk (closed to passengers from November 5 1956). All that remained by April 4 1986 (below right) was the double track line from Wigan and even this merged into single track (to Kirkby) just beyond the signal box. *John Marshall/PDS.*

SUCH was the prosperity of Liverpool Docks in the early part of this century that four pre-Grouping Companies enjoyed terminal facilities there — the Midland, Lancashire & Yorkshire, London & North Western and Cheshire Lines Committee systems all had goods depots in the area. The older view (right, above) shows the CLC yard at Bankfield as it was on March 1 1964, complete with a rake of insulated vans, just ten months before closure. When the modern picture was taken on April 2 1986 (right, below) the site of Bankfield yard was being filled with the demolished remains of other redundant examples of Liverpool's past. *John Marshall/PDS.*

LIVERPOOL EXCHANGE was the LYR terminus in the city, and once had a full complement of passenger services to Southport, Preston and the north, Wigan, Bolton, Manchester and beyond. Above: Stanier class 5MT 4-6-0 No. 44950 is seen on Sunday May 19 1968, ready to take the empty stock of the daytime Glasgow-Liverpool express to Kirkdale carriage sidings. Services were progressively withdrawn, and on April 30 1977 the entire station was closed and replaced by more modest facilities at Moorfields. The modern view shows the same location on April 1 1986 — with not a single trace of the railway remaining. *W. H. Ashcroft/PDS.*

RIVERSIDE station was originally built in 1895 by the Mersey Docks & Harbour Board to provide a direct passenger link between the LNWR system and Liverpool's Princes Landing Stage. After World War II most of the Trans-Atlantic passenger liner traffic was transferred to Southampton, and Riverside station gradually fell into disuse, finally closing in February 1971. Above on June 13 1964, LMS 'Jinty' 0-6-0T No. 47487 is seen a Riverside with a 'Liverpool Suburban' railtour, whils the lower view, on April 1 1986, shows the station struc ture to be remarkably intact, although the trackbed ha been filled. *Ian G. Holt/PDS.*

Above: A truly classic photograph of Stanier three-cylinder 'Jubilee' 4-6-0 No. 45646 *Napier* storming out of Liverpool Lime Street station with a Hull express, comprised of a mixture of LMS and BR standard Mk 1 coaching stock. Left: The present day scene at Lime Street is represented by 'Peak' diesel-electric No. 45146, departing with the 1005 to Scarborough on April 2 1986. Notice the platform extension, carried out during station alterations implemented at the time of electrification. *Eric Treacy (courtesy P. B. Whitehouse)/PDS.*

LIVERPOOL CENTRAL was the CLC's terminus in that city, and survived until the last-remaining Gateacre trains were withdrawn on April 17 1972. Top: Stanier '5MT' 4-6-0 No. 45256 awaits departure with the 1.15pm to Sheffield via Manchester Central, on May 27 1963, one of the few remaining steam-worked expresses from Liverpool Central at that time. The lower picture shows the same scene on April 1 1986, with the land still in BR ownership but in use as a Stores Depot, the trains long gone. Only the overbridge remains as a common factor, to positively identify the location. *Ian G. Holt/PDS.*

Above: On February 22 1964, a Liverpool Central-Gateacre DMU approaches Garston station, still fully signalled with semaphores, and including a CLC lower quadrant signal on the right. For a period of six years from 1972 (when Liverpool Central-Gateacre passenger services ended) this line was closed, until on January 3 1978 it was re-opened as part of the new electrified link from Garston to the Southport, Ormskirk and Kirkby lines. Thus on April 2 1986 (below), class 508 EMU No. 508126 is seen arriving on the 1050 Southport-Hunts Cross working. It is reassuring to see a suburban route which has been modernised and developed, rather than closed and abandoned. *Ian G. Holt/PDS.*

WARRINGTON
&
WINWICK

THE LNWR operated two rail-ways through Warrington, running at right angles to each other and with the Bank Quay station situated at their intersection. Above: The low level platforms at Bank Quay are illustrated, with Riddles 2-6-2T No. 84000 propelling a Manchester-Ditton Junction push-and-pull train of June 24 1961, and with the canopies of the high level platforms (on the West Coast Main Line) visible in the background. Right: The same location seen from a slightly higher viewpoint on February 22 1986. No trace remains of the low level station, which closed in September 1963, although the tracks are used by MGR coal trains to and from Fiddlers Ferry power station. Close inspection of the backdrop will show that considerable changes have taken place to the industrial landscape of the town. *John Marshall/JCH.*

WHILST the low level lines at Warrington see passengers no more, the upper part of Bank Quay station is as busy as ever, and served by a good number of West Coast Main Line expresses. One such is illustrated (above) as class 86 No. 86405 arrives with the 0620 Birmingham New Street-Lancaster, on June 7 1986. The upper photograph shows the same scene as it was on October 5 1963, with Stanier 'Princess Coronation' 4-6-2 No. 46251 *City of Nottingham* heading an RCTS tour from Crewe to Carlisle, composed mainly of LMS stock. Semaphore signals were removed and the signal box closed when the Warrington power signalling scheme was inaugurated in 1972 as a prelude to electrification of the Anglo-Scottish main line. *Ian G. Holt/JCH.*

Above: In sunny weather on January 1 1966, Stanier class 8F 2-8-0 No. 48408 passes Winwick Quay sidings on the up slow line with a mixed freight comprised of vans, tanks and a variety of open mineral wagons of steel and wooden bodied construction. The later view (right) depicts Winwick Quay on February 22 1986 as Class 86 No. 86249 passes on the up slow with a steel coil train. The four track main line survives, but the crossovers, signals, signal box and sidings have disappeared whilst industrial and road developments have spread across the once-open fields. *Dr. J. Gordon Blears/JCH.*

THE
WIGAN
AREA

Above: In the heart of the once-prosperous Lancashire coalfield, class G2 LNWR 0-8-0 No. 49438 heads north from Golborne with a loaded train including both steel and wooden-bodied wagons, on August 24 1961. It is sad to relate that as this book was being prepared only three Lancashire pits produced railborne coal — Bold, Parkside and nearby Bickershaw. Left: On April 9 1986 a breakdown train passes Golborne in the care of class 20s Nos. 20135 and 20008, bound for Springs Branch. *R. S. Greenwood/PDS.*

Right: Heading south through the rather dilapidated Wigan North Western station in 1966 is Stanier class 5 4-6-0 No. 44675, with a mixed freight train including a number of cattle wagons. The station was extensively modernised in 1971-2, and the new facilities were opened by the Mayor of Wigan in July 1972. The lower picture, dated April 3 1986, shows class 25/9 No 25904 with was then the latest generation of mixed freight - the 1338 Preston Deepdale-Warrington Walton Old Junction 'Speedlink' service (6F81), conveying empty cement and coal wagons. In the bay stands a two-car Class 108 DMU, waiting to form the 1316 service to Liverpool Lime Street. *Tom Heavyside/PDS.*

IN the 31 years which separate these two photographs, Wigan Wallgate station has undergone little change except for the replacement (and shortening!) of the platform canopy. Even the 'through' lines on both sides of the station remain in use. Above: BR Standard '4MT' 4-6-0 No. 75019 prepares to depart with the 11.00am Rochdale-Liverpool service on August 26 1955. Left: A two-car Class 108 DMU forms the 1510 Manchester Victoria-Kirkby train at the same location on April 9 1986. *Brian Morrison/PDS.*

THE much-changed scene at Hindley, where the 'Wigan avoiding line' (a loop off the WCML between Standish Junction and Bamfurlong Junction) crossed the east-bound main line from Wigan, to Bolton and Manchester. Top: The view at Hindley No. 2 signalbox, looking towards Wigan, on June 15 1968. The train is the daily Bamfurlong-Halliwell freight which at that time was booked for diesel haulage, with a steam banker, from Bamfurlong to De Trafford Junction. The train then reversed to join the Wigan-Bolton line at Hindley No. 2, with the consequence that the steam engine, in this case Stanier '5MT' No. 45104 became the train engine. The diesel locomotive (a class 40 just visible beyond the brake van) was providing banking assistance for the three miles of 1 in 97 to Westhoughton. Above: The Wigan avoiding line closed in 1974 and Hindley's extensive layout, its signal box and the impressive semaphore gantry have disappeared, to leave a plain double track section, while bushes and shrubs reclaim the former trackbed. On April 4 1986 Class 20s Nos. 20041 and 20106 pass with 6P82, the 0755 Warrington Walton Old Junction — Chorley freight. *Dr. J. Gordon Blears/PDS*.

AMIDST the maze of LNWR lines to the south of Wigan, the Great Central Railway operated its own route from Glazebrook to Lowton St. Mary's, from where branches led to Wigan Central and St. Helens. Above: Stanier 2-6-4T No. 42456 arrives at Lowton St. Mary's with the 4.41pm service from Wigan Central to Manchester Central on August 11 1963, 11 years after the St. Helens branch had lost its passenger service, and only 15 months before remaining passenger trains were withdrawn. By April 3 1986, as illustrated below, the bridge had been filled in and the location is barely recognisable. It is interesting to note how five carriages offering about 500 seats were used latterly for a lightly-used branch train, compared with the standard 130-seater Class 150 diesel units introduced latterly for middle and longer distance services elsewhere! *Ian G. Holt/PDS.*

RAILWAYS AROUND
BOLTON

Above: This view of the LYR's Horwich station was taken on April 1 1961. The train closest to the camera is the 12.15pm (Saturdays only) to Blackrod with 2-6-4T No. 42545, whilst in front of it is the 12.10pm (SO) to Manchester Victoria headed by 2-6-4T No. 42630. The Horwich branch is still used by freight trains serving the remaining facilities at the BREL works, but passen-ger services were withdrawn on September 27 1965 after many years of poor patronage — indeed the princi-pal users are understood to have been railway employ-ees travelling on privilege tickets! The site has now been levelled and made into an attractive recreation area, though the cobbled station approach remained in-situ on April 5 1986. *Hugh Ballantyne/PDS.*

Left: Arriving at Lostock Junction station on June 2 1965 is Stanier 2-6-4T No. 42647 with an evening Rochdale-Southport train. This station had four platforms, being situated in the fork of the Wigan and Preston lines, and was closed on November 7 1966. The lower view shows the 1710 Manchester Victoria-Kirby DMU at the same location on April 22 1986, with the original LYR box still controlling the junction despite rationalisation of the layout and the removal of some semaphores. Since then a new station has been built to the left of the picture with platforms only on the Bolton to Preston line, to serve recent housing developments. *John Marshall/ PDS.*

BOLTON retained much of its period charm when the older photograph (top) was taken just south of the station on June 18 1983, as class 25 No. 25042 is seen heading a typically lengthy train of empty newspaper vans bound for Red Bank carriage sidings. Since then, however, the goods yard was closed and lifted, the main running lines rationalised, the semaphore signalling removed and the fine LMS goods warehouse demolished, as shown in the lower view of class 47 No. 47636 with the same van duty on April 10 1986. *Both PDS.*

Above: Bolton steam shed lasted until June 1968, when after closure much of its stores and equipment went to the Keighley & Worth Valley Railway. The shed was mainly concerned with freight work and only local passenger services, but it also received locomotives from overhaul at Horwich Works for running-in duties. Latterly, the allocation consisted of Stanier 'Black 5s', '8F' 2-8-0s and a few '2MT' 2-6-0s. The older scene was photographed on August 6 1966, as a train spotter cycled round the shed. The lower picture shows the same spot on April 5 1986 — being re-developed as a housing estate and only recognisable with the aid of a large scale Ordanance Survey map!   *R.S. Greenwood/PDS.*

THE Bolton & Leigh Railway was actually the first line in Lancashire to be opened for the conveyance of public goods traffic, the official date being August 1828. The line had no connection with the LYR route through Bolton and its decline began in 1954 with the withdrawal of regular passenger trains and closure of the terminus at Great Moor Street. Crook Street goods yard survived another decade until April 26 1965 and it is pictured here with 0-6-0T No. 47430 in attendance on April 12 1962. Now there is no trace of the railway here, and the site is located only by the position of the Town Hall clock tower and a block of flats, as seen in the lower view, depicting the scene on February 23 1986. *John Marshall/PDS.*

BURY

Top: Knowsley Street station, Bury, is the setting for this view of Horwich 'Crab' 2-6-0 No. 42726, in far from steam-tight condition, leaving the platform with the two-coach Rochdale portion (detached at Bolton) of a morning Blackpool Central-Manchester express. This working was a hangover from the days when woollen and cotton industry magnates travelled each day from their homes on the Fylde coast to the cotton towns; first class accommodation always outnumbered second class facilities on this service. *R. S. Greenwood.*

Above: Passenger services from Bury Knowsley Street to Bolton and Rochdale were withdrawn from October 5 1970 and while the line remained open for coal traffic to Rawtenstall the station was razed to the ground. The station site is pictured here on February 23 1986, with the electrified tracks (subsequently changed to overhead wires for Metrolink trams) leading to the new bus/rail Interchange running across the picture. A level crossing was installed here when the new line was opened in 1980, but this was short-lived as the Rawtenstall coal traffic ceased in December of that year. *PDS.*

RADCLIFFE Black Lane station was situated on the Bolton-Bury line and survived until October 5 1970 when the last DMU services were withdrawn. Above: Riddles '2MT' 2-6-0 No. 78042 (allocated to Bank Hall) leaves the station with the 3.50 pm Rochdale-Wigan Wallgate stopping train, shortly before the diesel take-over. Right: The same location, abandoned and much overgrown, in April 1986. The town had two other main stations - Radcliffe Bridge on the now closed Clifton-Bury line, and Radcliffe Central, which was served by the 'Bury electrics' and is now on the Manchester to Bury Metrolink system. *B. K. Hilton/PDS.*

LCOMBE BROOK station, the terminus of a branch from Bury, is illustrated (below) with LYR Aspinall 2-2T No. 50651 having just arrived, May 4 1952, the last day of passenger services. The signal box, running loop and goods yard now seem unduly generous for such a minor branch line, but even more remarkable was the line's onetime electrification! The first scheme, with overhead supply, was inaugurated in 1913, but in 1918 the line was converted to third-rail working, which continued until 1951, and some third-rail fittings can be seen in the 1952 view. Holcombe Brook closed to goods in 1960, and by March 1986 (bottom) only a slight embankment on the right remained to mark the site of the station, now redeveloped as a shopping centre. *N.R. Knight/PDS.*

Above, left: The tidy and attractive station at Rawtenstall is pictured in April 1955, in the days when LYR 2-4-2Ts operated regular services between Bury and Bacup, and long before closure became a real threat. By 1970 however, the Bacup line had been closed for four years and the remaining line from Rawtenstall to Bury was singled, and on June 3 1972, the last DMU left Bury to the accompaniment of a chorus of detonators and a mourning party from Lancaster University, wearing appropriate dress. Above, right: The depressing remains of Rawtenstall station on March 2 1986, with one rusty track still in position, and with preservation hopes set high for eventual re-opening by the East Lancashire Railway Preservation Society. *N.R. Knight/PDS.*

WATERFOOT was an intermediate station between Rawtenstall and Bacup, surviving until the line's closure on December 5 1966. Right, above: An original 79xx series 'Derby lightweight' DMU, allocated to Bury, forms the 4.00pm Bacup-Bury service on March 26 1963, whilst on the road below a Rawtenstall Corporation Leyland bus heads for Bacup. Right, below: The derelict site of Waterfoot station on March 2 1986, with only the bus service still operating, now in the hands of a 1980-built 'Atlantean'. *I.G. Holt/PDS.*

ACUP was once the terminus for two routes, from both ochdale and Bury (via Rawtenstall). Long after with-rawal of the Rochdale service (June 16 1947), the Bury ne became one of the first in the country to go over to MU operation on February 6 1956. The upper picture lows an early afternoon DMU departure for Bury on June 10 1966, six months before closure of the line to Rawtenstall on December 5 1966, and after all signalling had been removed east of Stacksteads. In the yard is Stanier 'Black 5' 4-6-0 No. 44728 on a pick-up goods from Bury. The lower view shows the re-developed station area on January 26 1986. *Ian G. Holt./PDS.*

WHITWORTH lay on the LYR Rochdale-Bacup branch, and had already been closed to passenger services for 13 years when Riddles 'WD' 2-8-0 No. 90568 was pictured (above) with the daily coal trip on July 15 1960. Because of the severe gradients on the line, the maximum load was only 17 laden coal wagons for this powerful class of engine. The railway was progressively cut back and the last section, from Whitworth to Rochdale, was closed completely on August 21 1967. Right: The same view on March 2 1986, by which time some stretches of the line had been converted into a roadway. *R.S.Greenwood/ PDS.*

ROCHDALE & OLDHAM

Above: A photograph rich in the atmosphere and equipment of both industrial Lancashire and the steam railway, depicting the north end of Rochdale station in June 1967 when steam workings from Eastern Region depots were still a regular occurrence. Stanier 2-6-4T No. 42616, allocated to Low Moor shed, takes water in platform 2 after bringing in an afternoon parcels train from Bradford, and before returning home light-engine. By May 1 1986 the bay was no longer used by the Bacup trains for which it was intended, but survived for a few terminating DMUs from Manchester, via Rochdale. The signalling and some of the surrounding buildings are long gone as the 1532 York-Manchester Victoria DMU heads south on the main line (left). *R. S. Greenwood/PDS.*

Top: Approaching Castleton station on June 3 1960 is a Bank Holiday relief train from York to Manchester in the hands of Fleetwood '5MT' No. 45107. The scene is enhanced by Magee Marshall's maltings on the right and Tweedales and Smalley's textile machinery works on the left, whilst the pre-Grouping LYR shunting signal is also worthy of note. Above: A lone semaphore signal survived at this location on May 1 1986 as class 56 No 56070 headed south with the Leeds-Stanlow oil empties (7M35). *R. S. Greenwood/PDS.*

Above: Fairburn 2-6-4T No. 42284 stands in the wooden-decked branch platform at Middleton Junction with a train for Oldham in October 1954, by which time the passenger service was infrequent and had only another four years to run before withdrawal. Closure of the Oldham line to freight followed in October 1963, and the remaining main line platforms at Middleton Junction lost their passenger service in January 1966. The lower photograph shows the same scene on March 8 1986, with Middleton Junction signal box still signalling the main line, and one track in the foreground leading to Chadderton coal concentration depot. *N. R. Knight/PDS.*

NEW HEY coal yard is the location for this view (above) of LYR 'A' class 0-6-0 No. 52141, shunting the Saturday morning trip working from Royton Junction on May 28 1960. The engine crew seem concerned about the security of the side of a 3-plank wagon. The lower photograph shows new GMC-liveried class 142 unit No. 142008 on a Rochdale-bound service on January 25 1986. The sidings have long disappeared and the line between Shaw and Rochdale was singled on July 6 1980. *R.S. Greenwood/ PDS.*

Left: Class 142 DMU No 142007 passes the unstaffed halt at Royton Junction with the 1430 Shaw-Manchester Victoria service on March 8 1986 amidst much abandoned railway land. Subsequently the halt itself closed, since Derker station, opened in 1985, is more conveniently situated. This was a much busier scene in June 1956 (below) as Stanier '5MT' No 44890 passed with an evening Rochdale-Manchester Victoria (via Oldham) train. Diverging to the left is the branch to Royton, opened in 1864 and closed in 1966, whilst on the right is a thriving goods yard, with a Fowler '7F' 0-8-0 on pilot duty. This locomotive would have been kept busy all day at this time. *PDS/ Jim Davenport.*

Above: The neatly kept Oldham Ashton & Guide Bridge station at Oldham Clegg Street is pictured here, with class C13 4-4-2T No. 67438 (left) on a train from Guide Bridge and LMR '3MT' 2-6-2T No. 40056 on a Delph train in May 1953. This station was opened in 1861 and closed on May 4 1959, and over the years it enjoyed through services to both Euston and Kings Cross stations in London. Nothing now remains of the OA&GB route, but trains still pass the site of the adjacent Central station on the LYR line, as shown in the lower view of 'Pacer' unit No. 142001 on a morning Rochdale train on March 8 1986. *J. Davenport/PDS.*

Top: the 'Delph Donkey' is pictured here calling at Lees station, between Oldham and Greenfield, in the care of BR 2-6-2T No. 84012 in April 1955. The picturesque name of this train was derived from the fact that originally the Delph branch was worked by a single horse-drawn coach. In later years it was hauled by various LNWR tanks, and for a brief period steam railcars were tried. Since closure of the Oldham — Greenfield line on April 12 1964, much of the route has been made into a walkway, as illustrated in the lower photograph, dated March 8 1986. Introduced in 1953, these class 2 2-6-2s were extinct by 1965; No. 84012 was withdrawn in October 1963 and scrapped at Crewe works the same month. *J. Davenport/PDS.*

Above: At Delph station in May 1953, Fowler 2-6-2T No. 40057 awaits departure with the 1.55 pm railmotor train to Oldham Clegg Street. The branch enjoyed a brief spell of fame in June 1960 when the royal train, conveying H.M. Queen Elizabeth II, was stabled on its metals over-night, but even then its days were numbered, since regular passenger trains had gone for five years (service withdrawn May 2 1955) and total closure of the branch followed on November 4 1963. Next to the advertisement for Pale-thorpes sausages on the platform wall is a smaller enamel advert which proclaims: 'Virol — Anaemic girls need it'. Today, the station building still stands, having served various purposes including a sauna! The goods yard is used by Saddle-worth Council as an engineer's yard, and part of the railway has been used for a footpath. the lower picture was taken on January 24 1986 and shows several pre-served railway vehicles standing on a short length of track. *Jim Davenport/JCH.*

Nearly 90 years separate these two views of Dobcross Viaduct, near Saddleworth, and surprisingly few changes have taken place in the setting. Even the station building, just beyond the viaduct, survives, although the platforms disappeared soon after closure in 1968. The upper view dates back to the turn of the century, and shows an LNWR Webb 2-4-0 on a westbound 'mixed' train. In typical LNWR fashion, the locomotive would have been an 1890s re-build of an original machine already 40 years old: in its new guise, the last member of the class was not withdrawn until 1933. The lower view shows class 47 No. 47485 with the 1253 Scarborough-Bangor express on June 14 1986. Since then loco-hauled passenger services on the Trans-Pennine route have been completely phased out, and trains between Liverpool/Manchester and the North East are formed of three-car class 158 'Express' units. *Peter Fox Collection/PDS.*

UPPERMILL station was situated on the so-called Micklehurst line between Stalybridge and Diggle, built to relieve congestion on the main route and skirting the hills on the other side of the valley. It lost its local passenger service as early as 1917, though freight trains continued to use the Stalybridge end of the route until 1972. Top: 'WD' 8F 2-8-0 No. 90671 heads west with the 5.55pm Diggle-Heaton Norris goods, in July 1957.

Uppermill goods depot, seen on the left, was quite busy in the 1940s and early 1950s with traffic originating from the Admiralty Stores Depot, and until the early 1960s a fitted-freight actually started there. Above: the same location is pictured on July 18 1986, with Saddleworth Swimming Baths now occupying part of the former goods yard. *Jim Davenport/JCH.*

DIGGLE has declined over the years from being a busy junction (for the northern end of the Micklehurst 'loop') with freight yard, to providing just a crossover and loop. Above: 'Austerity' 2-8-0 No 90671 is seen departing with the 11.00 am goods to Oldham Glodwick Road, one of a number of freight services which once originated or called here, in September 1959. Left: Class 47 No. 47002 heads west with the 0830 Haverton Hill-Folly Lane ICI tanks (6M26) on January 24 1986. This working was one of the small number of freight trains not diverted via the LYR route. *Jim Davenport/ JCH.*

Above: Taking the Oldham Line at OA&GB Junction, just west of Ashton station, is Fairburn 2-6-4T No 42115 with the 12.34 pm (SO) Stockport-Oldham Clegg Street in August 1958. It was at this point that the OA&GB route joined briefly the LYR Manchester-Stalybridge line, seen in the bottom left-hand corner of the picture. Under the bridge the left-hand route continued to Guide Bridge. Right: The same scene on July 24 1986, with 'Peak' No 45133 heading east on the 1003 Liverpool-Newcastle express. The tall LYR signal box has been replaced by the modern BR standard version, and whilst the Guide Bridge line remained officially open at that time, it was very rarely used. *Jim Davenport/JCH.*

AROUND STOCKPORT

Above: This fine array of LNWR lower quadrant signals was located at Heaton Norris Junction, where the Manchester and Guide Bridge lines diverge just north of Stockport Edgeley viaduct. LMS 'Royal Scot' 4-6-0 No. 6115 *Scots Guardsman* is seen with a Euston-Manchester London Road express in June 1954. The modern picture (below) taken on March 8 1986, shows the LNWR goods warehouse still in use, though no longer connected to the railway. Since May 1984, HST units have operated under the wires to Piccadilly, and the example illustrated here is the 1050 from Paignton. *Jim Davenport/JCH.*

Right: Two views of the north end of Stockport Edgeley station, photographed from an incoming train on the up slow line. Top: In Summer 1958, a 'Patriot' 4-6-0 stands in the main down platform, whilst Fowler 2-6-4T No. 42379 shunts the yard (right), and a Stanier 2-6-4T waits in one of the station's through roads. In the modern picture, 28 years later, the trackwork remains basically unchanged except for the removal of the up-side bay and one of the down bay lines, whilst the other bay remains in use for the trains to Stalybridge. The colour-light signalling would have only recently been installed when the earlier photograph was taken, but is now considered outdated, with three signal boxes situated within a mile of each other. *Martin Welch/JCH.*

Left: At the south end of Edgeley station, an LNWR 'Super D' 0-8-0 heads north with a mixed goods train during 1956, whilst '8F' 2-8-0 No. 48506 stands in the main up platform. *Martin Welch.*

Top: Passing the site of Tiviot Dale station, on the CLC route through Stockport, class 37 No. 37251 heads west with a mixed freight conveying mineral wagons and empty 'Covhops'. Note the remains of one of the platforms, in the undergrowth to the left of the locomotive. The lower picture of this much-changed scene shows that by 28 April 1995 the railway has disappeared completely. After the 1939-45 war there was a regular service from Tiviot Dale to Liverpool Central via Cheadle as well as to Manchester Central and Chinley. The last passenger trains were withdrawn on March 6 1967, however, and the line between Cheadle Junction and Woodley saw its last through freight services in summer 1980. A long siding remained latterly in use from Woodley to Portwood Drops for stone traffic, but this was cut back to a new terminal near Bredbury in summer 1986. *Tom Heavyside/JCH.*

Top: Stanier '8F' 2-8-0 No. 8089 heads a train of ICI limestone hoppers through the CLC station at Cheadle in June 1939, en-route from Tunstead, near Buxton, to Northwich. This same freight service continues to operate in 1986, and an evening train is pictured (above) on June 19, with class 20s Nos. 20302 and 20308 in charge.

Even the wagons have hardly altered during these 3 years. Passenger services were withdrawn on January 1967, the platforms have been removed, the line ha been singled, and the station buildings converted fo use as a restaurant. *W. Potter/PDS.*

DIDSBURY station is pictured (above) in July 1954, with 'Compound' 4-4-0 '4P' No. 40927 (allocated to Derby) calling with the 2.42 pm Manchester Central-Derby service. Notice the MR lower quadrant signals with sighting boards at the end of the down platform. By March 17 1986 (left), 19 years after the line was closed (January 2 1967), the site was heavily overgrown, although surprisingly the platforms remained in situ. *N. R. Knight/JCH.*

ROMILEY was once the location of a three-way junction, operated jointly by the Great Central and Midland Railways. Above: Stanier 'Jubilee' 4-6-0 No. 45581 *Bihar and Orissa* takes the Reddish line at Romiley with the empty stock for a return Belle Vue-West Riding excursion on May 31 1966. The lines on the right led down the incline past Bredbury to Stockport Tiviot Dale and were closed less than a year after this photograph was taken.

Below: On February 22 1986 the left-hand route t Guide Bridge remained open, as did the direct route t Manchester, via Reddish. Class 31 No. 31431 heads th 1208 Hull-Manchester Piccadilly past Romiley. Since th opening of the Hazel Grove chord, most of these lon distance services have since been diverted vi Stockport, primarily to attract additional traffic. *Ian I Smith/JCH.*

Top: Altrincham EMU depot is pictured on June 20 1970, less than a year before its closure. It serviced the 1500V dc electric multiple units which lasted in every-day operation from 1931 until conversion of the line to 25kV ac on May 3 1971. The building in the distance is the original terminus of the Manchester South Junction & Altrincham Railway at Bowdon, closed when the CLC was opened between Altrincham and Chester and the present Altrincham station was brought into use. The lower view shows an almost deserted car park on the abandoned site on March 29 1986. *John Marshall/JCH.*

MANCHESTER

Top: Stanier '8F' 2-8-0 No. 48692 heads a westbound unfitted coal train through Eccles station on August 11 1967. At that time, this LNWR approach to Manchester was still quadruple track, but now only the former fast lines remain in situ for through trains, with just one slow line retained for use as a headshunt by oil trains reversing down to the terminal at Weaste. The terraced houses on the left were demolished to make way for the M602 motorway. Above: A class 108 DMU calls at Eccles on the 1521 Chester-Manchester Victoria service on April 22 1986. *A. Wyn Hobson/JCH*

Above: Departing past the overhead signal box at Manchester London Road station is 'Britannia' 4-6-2 No. 70032 *Tennyson* with a London Euston express in 1955. London Road remained a joint station until Nationalisation, with even a ticket barrier on the footbridge connecting the LMS (LNWR) and LNER (GCR) sections. The latter section once enjoyed through services to Marylebone, and was also the first part of the station to be electrified, in 1954, at 1500V dc for the Woodhead line. Upon re-modelling in 1959, the station was renamed Piccadilly. The extended platforms and 25kV electrification are shown in the lower view of the 1008 DMU from Buxton arriving on February 18 1986. *Eric Treacy (courtesy P.B. Whitehouse)/JCH.*

CENTRAL station was the Midland Railway terminus at Manchester, and was used in later years by the CLC, jointly operated by the LMS and LNER. Yet another London service ran from here, via the Midland route, to St. Pancras, as well as services to Liverpool Central and Chester Northgate. Its rundown began on March 6 1967, when local services on the Midland line were withdrawn. Then, on January 1 1968 the expresses to Derby and London were diverted to Piccadilly, and Central's final closure was marked by the diversion of Liverpool and Chester services to Oxford Road on May 5 1969. Above: The station's cavernous interior in 1956. Below: The same scene following conversion as the G-MEX Exhibition Centre 30 years later. *Eric Oldham/Peter McCormack Photography.*

Above: The familiar frontage of Central station is pictured on April 16 1969, less than a month before closure, when it cost 2/6 for passengers to park their cars, and 5/- for non rail-users. One of the posters to the right of the gate advertises a weekend in London, including fare and hotel, for £8/17/6! Left, above: The same view on March 17 1986. The station was used for many years after closure as an NCP car park before finally being converted into the fine and much-needed G-MEX building, its full title being the 'Greater Manchester Exhibition and Event Centre. *John Marshall/JCH.*

Left, below: The 'temporary' wooden frontage buildings built by the Midland Railway in 1880, which in fact survived the closure of Central and are seen here in 1982 when the station was being used as a car park. *Tom Heavyside.*

Top: Stanier '5MT' 4-6-0 No. 45290 approaches Manchester Victoria from Queens Road sidings with the empty stock for a Fleetwood express in May 1961. At this time re-signalling was in progress, and the new East signal box can be seen under construction on the left of the picture. Below: A class 142 DMU approaches the statio on 15 April 1994 over a very different track layout. Th platform from which the original picture was taken ha been shortened, necessitating the slightly differen viewpoint. *Jim Davenport/JCH.*

Above: At the west end of Manchester Exchange, on August 18 1962, Horwich 'Crab' 2-6-0 No. 42758 is in charge of a Southport train on the through line from Victoria, whilst a BR Standard 4-6-0 No. 73132 stands in a stabling siding. Manchester Exchange was the LNWR terminal in the city, having services to Chester General and North Wales, Liverpool Lime Street and Wigan North Western via Tyldesley. Together with the LYR's Victoria station, it shared the longest platform in Britain, built after the two companies became amalgamated in the 1923 Grouping. Even 17 years after closure and subsequent demolition, some of Exchange's platforms survived, as shown in the lower view of No. 56061 heading the 1018 Leeds-Stanlow oil empties (7M54) on May 27 1986. *J.S. Whiteley/PDS.*

PASSENGER trains continued using Manchester Exchange until May 5 1969, when services were diverted to Victoria, although the fine overall roof survived for more than a decade after that time. Top: An eastbound 'Trans-Pennine' DMU prepares to depart from Exchange on August 25 1968, whilst a Metropolitan Cammell unit stands in the left-hand platform. Above: The tracks have now gone completely from the old Exchange end of Victoria, as seen in this view dated 1? April 1994. *G. W. Morrison/JCH.*